KIDS CAN COOK

CONTENTS

A READ-ABOUT

PIZZA SNACKS

INGREDIENTS

2 hamburger buns

slices of salami

¼ cup of tomato sauce

slices of cheese

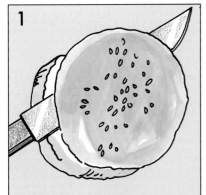

1 Cut buns in half, if necessary.

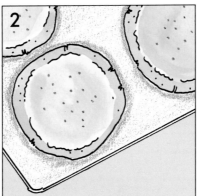

2 Toast buns lightly in oven. Leave oven on.

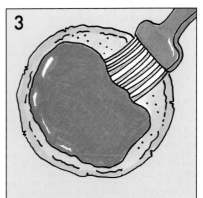

3 Spread tomato sauce on each half.

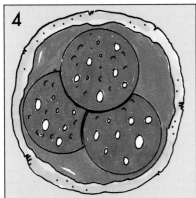

4 Top each with slices of salami.

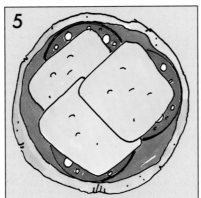

5 Cover with slices of cheese.

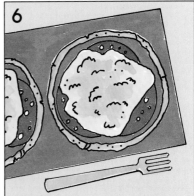

6 Put back in oven. Toast until cheese bubbles.

MICROWAVE
GINGERBREAD FACES

4

INGREDIENTS

120 grams (5 ounces) very soft butter

¾ cup brown sugar

4 tablespoons golden syrup (molasses)

2 cups flour

1 teaspoon baking soda
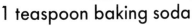

1 tablespoon ground ginger

Decorations for faces

1
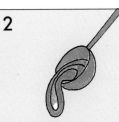
Beat butter and sugar until soft and creamy.

2
Add golden syrup (or molasses) and mix well.

3

Add flour, baking soda, and ginger. Mix well.

4

Sprinkle a little flour on a cold surface.

5

Roll dough thinly. Cut into round shapes.

6
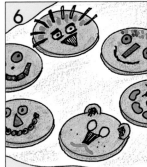
Put 6 on sheet of wax paper. Make faces.

7
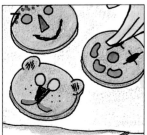
Place on turntable. Cook on High 2½ minutes.

8

Carefully lift out wax paper. Leave to cool.

KIDS CAN COOK
MICROWAVE
BAKED APPLES

INGREDIENTS

4 apples

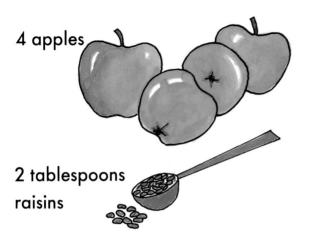

3 tablespoons
brown sugar

1 teaspoon cinnamon

2 tablespoons
raisins

4 teaspoons honey

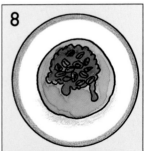

1

Scoop top
from apples.

2

Prick with fork.

3

Stand apples
in dish.

4

Mix raisins,
brown sugar,
and cinnamon.

5

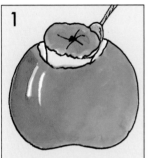

Press into each
apple.

6

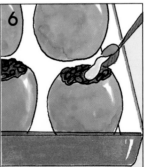

Put a teaspoon
of honey on top
of each.

7

Put a little
water into dish.
Put paper towel
on top.

8

Cook on High
10 minutes.
Spoon liquid
over apples.

7

TUNA ROLL

INGREDIENTS

1 bread roll

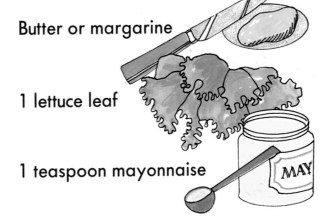

Butter or margarine

1 lettuce leaf

¼ cup drained tuna

1 teaspoon mayonnaise

1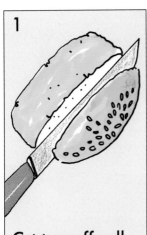
Cut top off roll.

2
Make a little hole in base.

3
Butter roll.

4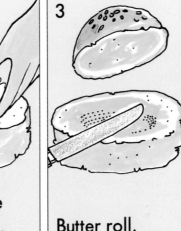
Put tuna and mayonnaise in bowl.

5
Mix together.

6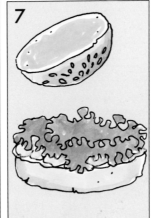
Put in roll.

7
Add lettuce.

8
Put top of roll on. Serve.

HOT CHOCOLATE

INGREDIENTS

1 cup milk

2 heaped teaspoons
chocolate drink mix

1 marshmallow

1 Put milk in mug.

2 Add chocolate drink mix. Stir well.

3 Microwave on High 80 seconds.

4 Stir. Put in marshmallow. Serve.

COOL LEMONADE

INGREDIENTS

½ lemon

½ cup sugar

2½ cups water

Ice cubes

1 mint leaf,
if you have one

1 Slice lemon thinly into bowl.

2 Add sugar. Mash with fork till mixed well.

3 Add water. Stir well. Pour into glass.

4 Remove lemon rind if wished. Add ice cubes and mint leaf.

BANANA DELICIOUS

INGREDIENTS

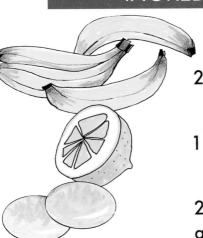

4 bananas

½ lemon

2 eggs

2 tablespoons sugar

1 cup coconut

2 tablespoons apricot jam

1

Turn oven to 180ºC (350ºF). Peel bananas.

2

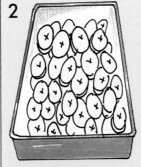

Slice bananas into ovenproof dish.

3

Squeeze lemon juice all over.

4

Put eggs and sugar in bowl. Beat well until creamy.

5

Stir in coconut and jam. Mix it all well.

6

Pour it evenly over bananas.

7

Bake for 25 minutes or until golden.

8

Serve warm with cream or ice cream.

CUPCAKES

INGREDIENTS

1 cup flour

1 teaspoon
baking powder

½ cup sugar

50 grams (2 ounces)
butter or margarine

½ cup milk

1 egg

1 teaspoon vanilla

Turn oven to
190ºC (375ºF).
Put paper liners
in muffin pans.

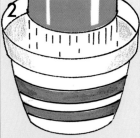

2

Sift flour,
baking powder,
and sugar into
bowl.

3

Put butter in
small pan.

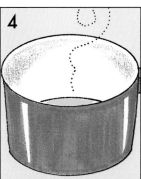

4

Melt gently—
don't boil it.

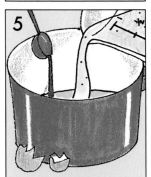

5

Take off heat.
Add milk, egg,
vanilla. Mix.

6

Pour into flour
mixture.
Mix well.

Spoon into
baking cups.
Fill ¾ full.

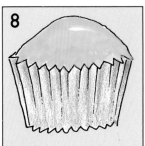

8

Bake 10–15
minutes until
risen and
golden.

DECORATING YOUR CUPCAKES

Now the fun begins! Spread the cooled cupcakes with icing (or frosting) and decorate the tops in lots of different ways.